★ HOCKEY SUPERSTARS ★

CONNOR McDAVID

BY NICOLE MORTILLARO

CAPSTONE PRESS
a capstone imprint

Sports Illustrated Kids Hockey Superstars are published by Capstone Press,
1710 Roe Crest Drive, North Mankato, Minnesota 56003.
www.capstonepub.com

Library of Congress Cataloging-in-Publication Data
Cataloging-in-Publication data can be found on the Library of Congress website.

ISBN 978-1-4914-9021-1 (library binding)
ISBN 978-1-4914-9026-6 (paperback)
ISBN 978-1-4914-9027-3 (eBook PDF)

Developed and Produced by Focus Strategic Communications, Inc.
Adrianna Edwards: project manager
Jennifer MacKinnon: editor
Rob Scanlan: designer and compositor
Mary Rose MacLachlan: media researcher
Wendy Scavuzzo: fact checker

Photo Credits
CHL Images: Aaron Bell, cover, back cover, 14, 20–21, 30–31(background), 32
(background), Terry Wilson, 7, 10; Getty Images: B Wippert, 22–23, Claus Andersen,
17, Steve Russell, 4; Newscom: Icon Sportswire/Bob Frid, 26–27, Icon Sportswire/
Curtis Comeau, 1, Polaris/Brendan Bannon, 13, 18–19, USA Today/Steve Mitchell, 29,
ZUMA Press/Frank Jansky, 24; Sports Illustrated: David E. Klutho, 9

Design Elements: Shutterstock

Printed in China.
072015   009103R

TABLE OF CONTENTS

McDavid (17) breaks away from Team Russia to score a goal in the gold-medal game.

CHAPTER 1

THE ONE TO WATCH

"This is our house!"

The words hung in the air. On the ice 22 young men in red and white skated around Toronto's Air Canada Centre. Gold medals hung around their necks.

Team Canada had just defeated the Russians 5-4. The 2015 International Ice Hockey Federation (IIHF) World Junior Championships were over. The joy felt by these young men was written across their faces. Laughing and hugging, they celebrated their gold-medal win.

Seventeen-year-old Connor McDavid was as happy as anyone. Josh Morrissey had sent him a fantastic pass in the second period. McDavid had collected it and gone on a **breakaway**. When he scored the crowd rose to its feet. The thundering cheers rang off the walls.

Everyone there knew who he was.

breakaway—a rush toward the net with no one but the goalie to stop the skater

McDavid has had many nicknames. He's been called "The Next One" and "The Exceptional One." The hockey world has watched him for years. When he was only 15 years old, people were already **anticipating** his **draft** into the National Hockey League (NHL). They compared him to "The Great One"— hockey legend Wayne Gretzky. They said that McDavid could be the "The Next One."

McDavid finished the junior championships with three goals and eight assists. That gave him 11 points. Most of those points came in the last three games. McDavid only got better as the tournament went on.

After taking a photo with his gold-medal-winning team, McDavid skated off the ice. But it wouldn't be his last time at the Air Canada Centre. He would return the next season in the NHL. The only question was, which team's jersey would he be wearing?

anticipate—to look forward to or to expect something

draft—to choose a person to join a sports organization or team

FAST FACT

McDavid almost missed the junior championships. He was playing for the Erie Otters and broke a bone in his hand. The injury kept him off the ice for five weeks. McDavid recovered just in time.

McDavid (center) celebrates the IIHF gold-medal win with his teammates.

CHAPTER 2

BORN TO SKATE

Connor McDavid's development as a hockey player started early. He was born January 13, 1997, and he grew up north of Toronto in Newmarket, Ontario.

McDavid's life in hockey began when he was a toddler. But his first experience on skates wasn't on the ice. It was in his basement. He was almost three years old, and he put on a pair of in-line skates. He began to skate around the basement. He never fell once.

By the time he was six, McDavid had been playing ice hockey for two years. He'd also outgrown his teammates. His parents tried to sign him up on a team of seven-year-olds. But the local hockey association wouldn't allow it.

Instead, McDavid joined a team in a nearby town. There he played against kids as old as nine. He was already a star.

FAST FACT

Though McDavid grew up near Toronto, his favorite team was the Pittsburgh Penguins. His favorite player was, of course, Sidney Crosby.

McDavid grew up watching Sidney Crosby and hoped to follow in the NHL star's footsteps.

McDavid was only 14 years old when he first joined the Toronto Marlboros.

As a young teenager, McDavid lived and breathed hockey. He was on the ice every day. At home he would set up obstacle courses on his driveway. They were made out of paint cans, skateboards, and hockey sticks. Wearing in-line skates, he'd jump some objects and carry the puck around others. He also practiced shots in the garage. Sometimes they'd be hard enough to put holes in the walls!

It was this dedication that had some people calling him a **perfectionist**. McDavid didn't want to be *good* at hockey. He wanted to be great.

McDavid played on AAA teams, the highest level in minor hockey. By 2011, he was playing for a Toronto Marlboros AAA team.

perfectionist—someone who wants things to be perfect

CUJO

When McDavid was about seven years old, he played lacrosse with Tristan Joseph. Tristan is NHL-great Curtis Joseph's son. The two boys became friends. They played together on the AAA York Simcoe Express hockey team. Sometimes Curtis Joseph, known as "Cujo," would invite the boys to his farm. They would play in "The Barn." Instead of animals or hay, this barn held an ice rink. There McDavid skated for hours and hours and improved his hockey skills. He also formed a bond with Cujo.

During the 2011–12 season with the Toronto Marlboros, McDavid racked up 79 goals and 130 assists for 209 points. The hockey league named him Player of the Year. He was only 15 years old, playing against boys who were 16 or 17 years old.

It was clear that McDavid's skill was beyond his years. He was ready for the Ontario Hockey League (OHL). But at 15 he was a year too young. He had to apply for **exceptional** player status.

McDavid was granted the special status. But he didn't let it go to his head. His **demeanor** on and off the ice didn't change. He remained humble and respectful.

exceptional—something that is rare or extraordinary

demeanor—the way someone behaves

FAST FACT

Only three other people have been given exceptional player status. They are John Tavares, Aaron Ekblad, and Sean Day. Tavares is now captain of the New York Islanders. Ekblad plays defense for the Florida Panthers. Day remains in the OHL.

Even as a young player, McDavid knew how to use his speed to score.

McDavid, seen here in 2013 with the Erie Otters, is known for his amazing ability to set up great scoring chances.

McDavid was drafted first overall by Erie, Pennsylvania's Otters. He joined the team for the 2012–13 season. He went on to score 25 goals in 63 games. Plus, he had 41 assists. For 15 games in a row, he got at least one point. At the end of the season, McDavid was named OHL Rookie of the Year. Though the Otters didn't make the playoffs, McDavid's talent was clear.

The Otters' General Manager, Sherwood Bassin, is a big fan of McDavid. "You build championships around players with this special ability," Bassin said. Bassin also said that McDavid has a "phenomenal **work ethic**."

work ethic—a belief in the value of hard work

FAST FACT

McDavid's 15-game point streak began with his second game in the OHL. By its end he had scored 8 goals and racked up 12 assists for 20 points.

CHAPTER 3

"THE NEXT ONE"

It was the second period in a game against the Plymouth Whalers. The score was 5-1 for the Erie Otters.

Otters' goalie Oscar Dansk kicked the puck out after a shot on net. It bounced off the boards. McDavid quickly picked it up. He gained speed as he headed toward the Whalers' end.

Whalers' **defenseman** Alex Peters was waiting. McDavid **stickhandled** the puck. His eyes were set on the goal. Peters tried to poke the puck out from McDavid, and then he tried to check him. Instead, McDavid faked to his left. He tucked the puck between Peters' legs and moved to the right.

Whalers' goalie Zack Bowman saw McDavid coming. Going down low Bowman tried to cover the net. But McDavid saw the opening on Bowman's stick side. He shot the puck in. Another goal for McDavid!

defenseman—a player who lines up in a defensive zone to prevent opponents from getting open shots on goal

stickhandle—to control and move the puck with a hockey stick

McDavid's great skill made him a superstar for the Erie Otters. Soon, many people wanted to wear the number 97.

McDavid's second season with the Otters had many similar highlight-reel plays. It was clear that a good player was getting even better. He had spent his summer training with hockey legend Gary Roberts. He'd worked hard and gained 20 pounds. McDavid was bigger, stronger, and faster.

Word spread about his incredible skill. He would show up to sold-out away games. Fans held up signs to cheer him on. He wasn't in the NHL, but McDavid was already a star. People wanted to see "The Next One" in action.

FAST FACT

McDavid wears the year of his birth, 97, on his jersey. Sidney Crosby does the same thing—87!

McDavid (green shirt) trained hard each day to get better and stronger.

McDavid's second season with the Otters was exceptional. In just 56 games he had 28 goals and 71 assists.

With McDavid's help the Otters made the playoffs that year. They advanced to the conference finals. McDavid had 4 goals and 15 assists. The Otters didn't win. But it was the best they'd done in years.

ANOTHER STAR

McDavid was at the top of many NHL scouting lists. But the scouts were also watching Jack Eichel. He was a center with Boston University in the National Collegiate Athletic Association. McDavid was a better playmaker. But Eichel was fast and powerful, and he had a great shot. Many people wondered if he'd be the first pick in the 2015 NHL draft.

McDavid's incredible plays helped the Otters get to the playoffs in 2014.

CHAPTER 4

ROAD TO THE NHL

The 2014–15 season was to be McDavid's last in the OHL. And what a season it was.

That September McDavid was named team captain. In November he began a 27-game point streak. By the time it ended in May, he'd scored 26 goals and had 32 assists. The Otters' faith in McDavid had been rewarded.

McDavid was living up to the hype. The last person to have a streak that long was former OHL star John Tavares. In the 2007–08 season Tavares had 15 goals and 39 assists during his 27-game point streak.

FAST FACT

On April 10, 2015, McDavid set another new record. He became the first Erie Otter to ever score five goals in one game!

McDavid's success continued into the 2014–15 season.

McDavid finished his career with the Otters with 166 regular-season games played, 97 goals, and 188 assists. He had a total of 285 points.

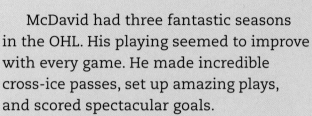

McDavid had three fantastic seasons in the OHL. His playing seemed to improve with every game. He made incredible cross-ice passes, set up amazing plays, and scored spectacular goals.

By April 2015 everyone knew McDavid was ready for the NHL. But he was still an Otter. He would lead his team to the playoffs one last time.

The Otters made it all the way through to the Rogers OHL Championship series. They lost to the Oshawa Generals in Game 5. But McDavid had been on fire throughout the playoffs. He had 21 goals, 28 assists, and 49 points in 20 playoff games. That made him third all-time in the OHL for points in a playoff season.

FAST FACT

McDavid was named the Most Valuable Player of the 2015 OHL playoffs and was given the Wayne Gretzky 99 Award.

MY REACTION WHEN WE DRAFT #MCDAVID

The Toronto Maple Leafs were hoping to add McDavid to their team.

The NHL's draft lottery was held in April 2015. In the days leading up to it, McDavid's name was everywhere. You couldn't turn on a sports show without seeing his face. McDavid seemed to be everyone's first choice. Which team would have the chance to pick him first?

McDavid's home team, the Toronto Maple Leafs, had a dismal 2014–15 season. Many Toronto fans hoped the team could draft the hockey **phenom**.

phenom—a young, unusually talented person

FAST FACT

Most low-ranking teams had their eyes on McDavid. Buffalo Sabres fans even had McDavid jerseys made!

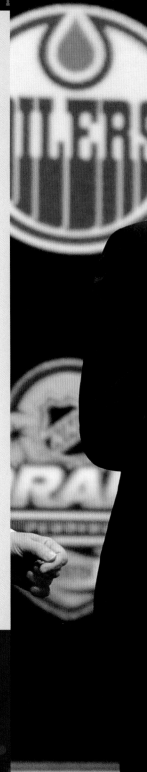

But Edmonton Oiler fans were the lucky winners. Their team won the draft lottery. It would get the first pick.

On draft day no one was surprised when the team called out McDavid's name. The crowd cheered. Smiling, McDavid pulled on the blue and orange sweater.

"Now I'm an Edmonton Oiler. I couldn't be more proud," McDavid said after the draft. "It's been a great day!"

Hockey fans are looking forward to seeing McDavid play in the NHL. They can't wait to see "The Next One" in action!

FAST FACT

Jack Eichel, who at one time many thought might be the number one pick in the 2015 NHL Draft, was chosen second overall by the Buffalo Sabres.

On June 26, 2015, Connor McDavid (right) was presented with a team jersey after being selected by the Edmonton Oilers as the number one overall pick in the 2015 NHL Draft.

GLOSSARY

anticipate (an-TIS-uh-peyt)—to look forward to or to expect something

breakaway (BREYK-uh-wey)—a rush toward the goal with no one but the goalie to stop the skater

defenseman (di-FENS-muhn)—a player who lines up in a defensive zone to prevent opponents from getting open shots on goal

demeanor (di-MEE-ner)—the way someone behaves

draft (DRAHFT)—to choose a person to join a sports organization or team

exceptional (ik-sep-SHuh-nl)—something that is rare or extra-special

perfectionist (per-FEK-shuh-nist)—someone who wants things to be perfect

phenom (FE-nom)—a young, unusually talented person

stickhandle (STIK-hand-ul)—to control and move the puck with a hockey stick

work ethic (WURK ETH-ik)—a belief in the value of hard work

READ MORE

Frederick, Shane. *Hockey Legends in the Making*. Sports Illustrated Kids: Legends in the Making. North Mankato, Minn.: Capstone Press, 2014.

Frederick, Shane. *Side-by-Side Hockey Stars: Comparing Pro Hockey's Greatest Players*. Sports Illustrated Kids: Side-by-Side Sports. North Mankato, Minn.: Capstone Press, 2015.

Zweig, Eric. *The Big Book of Hockey for Kids*. Toronto, Ontario: Scholastic Canada Ltd., 2013.

INTERNET SITES

FactHound offers a safe, fun way to find Internet sites related to this book. All of the sites on FactHound have been researched by our staff.

Here's all you do:

Visit *www.facthound.com*

Type in this code: 9781491490211

Super-cool stuff!

Check out projects, games, and lots more at
www.capstonekids.com

INDEX